William Henry Talley
(1847-1910)
A Life of Duty & Devotion

by William Alfred Talley, Jr.

Fluvanna Historical Society
Palmyra, Virginia
2012

Respectfully yours
April 14th 1905   Wm H Talley

Fluvanna History is the periodical of the Fluvanna Historical Society and presents a record of how the beliefs and actions of the people of "Old Flu" shaped history in the Virginia Midland and beyond. It is intended to promote historical research and writing to create among its readers a greater knowledge and understanding of Fluvanna heritage. For information about submitting manuscripts, please request and review the guidelines for authors (also found at www.fluvannahistory.org). Since 1965 this publication, originally titled *The Bulletin*, has been distributed to members of the Society and to other subscribers. To order additional copies of current and back issues and to make other inquiries, write to:

Fluvanna Historical Society • P. O. Box 8 • Palmyra, VA 22963

Published by Cedar Creek Publishing, Bremo Bluff, Virginia
on behalf of the Publications Committee
of the Fluvanna Historical Society

Library of Congress Control Number 2012946328

ISBN 978-0-9839192-5-4

CONTENTS

5

Foreword

This edition of *Fluvanna History* gives voice to a person who until now has remained a largely silent witness to an intense period in our collective history. His world tested him by war, sweeping economic and social uncertainties, and extended family obligations. His generation might have called it *sweet adversity* in which individuals gained strength and even a degree of wisdom through managing if not always conquering the trials and tribulations of their lives. The William Henry Talley story is about an honorable man, but a man of his times, who faced the challenges of his day and still achieved a reasonably happy life.

We thank Al Talley for researching and writing about his grandfather, and we are delighted to add this biography to the published history of "Old Flu." Members of the publications committee review and proofread each manuscript we publish, and the Society is ever appreciative of their contribution.

Edition Number 86 introduces a change in design from saddleback to perfect binding. The new format means no more rusty staples as editions age, accommodates longer or multiple manuscripts with up to 30 percent more printable pages and, we think, produces a more professional finish. This edition also includes the first Civil War text to be published during the commemoration of the war's 150th anniversary.

David Bearr
Publications Editor

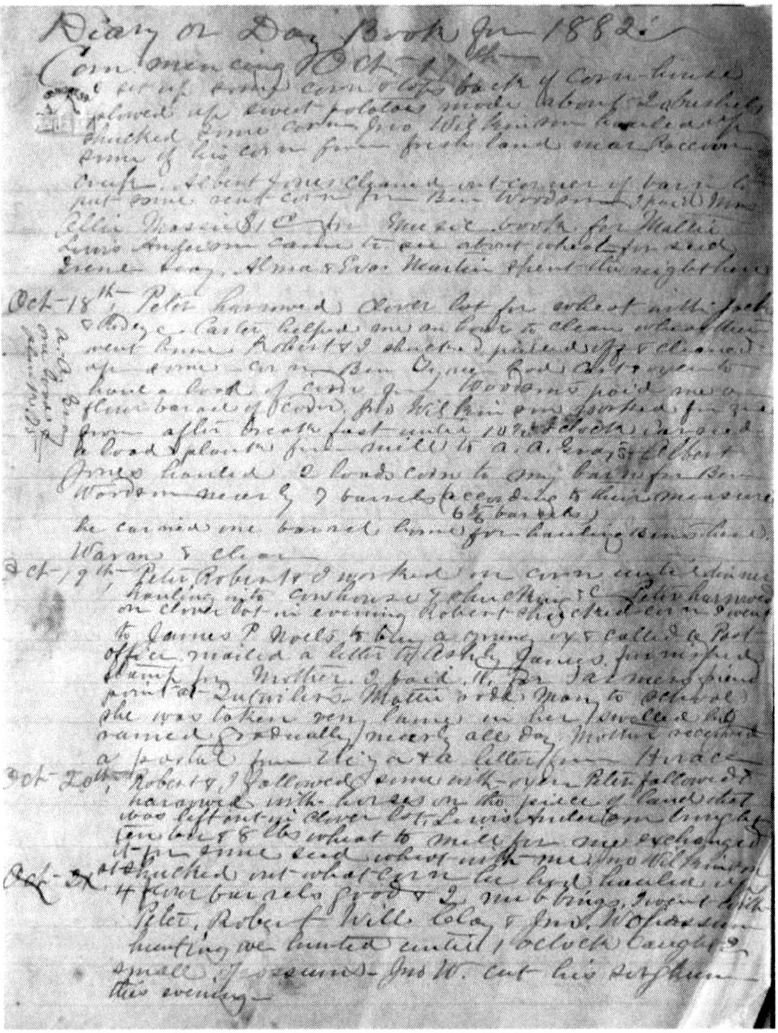
Diary or Day Book for 1882

Commencing Oct 17th

Oct 18th, Peter harrowed clover lot for wheat

Oct 19th, Peter, Robert & I worked on corn

Oct 20th, Robert & I fallowed

The Daybook

Preface
with Acknowledgments

I never saw myself writing a manuscript for the Fluvanna Historical Society. I have greatly enjoyed reading and learning from the publications by David Bearr, Ellen Miyagawa, Minnie Lee McGehee, and others; but creating one I thought was far beyond the capability of my short attention span. However, due to the interaction of several unexpected influences, I felt compelled to give it a try.

If you will follow with me through this story, it is due to the influence and assistance of two persons. The first is my genealogy-addicted wife Carolyn who has never met a family tree that did not challenge her to learn the story of each leaf. She started doing the research on my family and that finally shamed me into showing some interest. The second is David Bearr, who lent a 19th century daybook by some unknown author to Minnie Lee McGehee, who then passed it to Carolyn for purposes of transcription. As she undertook the task, it immediately became clear to us that the author was my grandfather William Henry Talley.

During our winter vacation to the Florida Keys, we chose a location where there was no television signal or internet access, so reading was our main avocation. Carolyn started work on transcribing the daybook, but it was hard to decipher the handwriting and then type it without losing her place, so I offered to read it to her as she typed. I felt that I got to know a great deal about my grandfather and his life at that time from his daily notes. I learned that David was considering using the daybook as the basis of a publication about life in Fluvanna in the 1880s, so I contacted him.

It would be ideal if all children could spend time with their grandparents. That generation has usually reached the stage in their lives when they appreciate just how short life is, and how important it is to spend time with children and answer their never-ending questions. Unfortunately, I did not have the opportunity to share the life of my paternal grandfather as he died some 34 years before my birth. I had learned the little that I know about him from the bit of history that I retained from his obituary printed in the *Midland Virginian*, from suit papers that I read in the Fluvanna County Clerk's Office, and from some of his possessions that I inherited.

However, reflecting on the daybook, I knew enough to recognize that it was written during such a brief period of his life, when he was engaged in basically subsistence farming, that anyone reading it alone would have no idea of the accomplishments and character of my grandfather. I emailed David and asked him if he would allow me to use portions of the daybook as a part of the story of the life of William Henry Talley, and would he be willing to help me with the project. He kindly agreed on both counts, so this endeavor began.

We are all indebted to Lynn Humphrey Knight of Florida who over a number of years has amassed and shared an impressive amount of documents related to the Talley and Shepherd families. She is a great-granddaughter of Eliza Shepherd Page, William Henry Talley's sister, and that means Lynn and I are Talley cousins. Perhaps less obvious is that on her Shepherd side of the house, she and David Bearr are also cousins.

Much appreciation is due Jamie Light. She is an internet contact who graciously located and provided information from the Bristow Center in Austin, Texas.

Judge William Alfred Talley, Jr. retired from the Sixteenth Judicial District Court of Virginia in 2004. He is a Fluvanna native and lifelong resident of Palmyra. His present home is located on the land his father W. A. Talley, Sr. farmed. His mother Eleanor Wright Talley was a highly regarded teacher in the county and is a charter member of the Fluvanna Historical Society. At one time mother and son served together as Society officers. His wife Carolyn Cason Talley is now a board member.

TALLEY GENEALOGY
Zachariah Talley (ca.1745 – 1832)
married:
(Date & Wife's Name Unknown)

William Peace	Charity
Jacky	Zachariah

William Peace Talley (1770-1849)
married 25 January 1798
Frances Daniel (1778-1842)

William D.	John Archer
Zachariah	Samuel
Edwin P.	Joseph H.
Martha	Horace Alfred

Horace Alfred Talley (1815-1878)
married 7 November 1844
Martha Quarles Wills (ca. 1825 - ca. 1904)

William Henry	Eliza Marie
Horace A.	Mattie Quarles Talley
	Mary L.

William Henry Talley (1847-1910)
married 21 November 1900
Mary E. Collins (1877-1954)

William Alfred	Virginia Quarles

William Alfred Talley, Sr. (1903-1985)
married 3 May 1935
Mary Eleanor Wright (1912- ____)

William Alfred Talley, Jr.

William Henry Talley
(1847-1910)
A Life of Duty and Devotion

Family History

You cannot really understand a person without some knowledge of the family. We are all a product of a combination of genetic and environmental influences, and family is the basis of both. So we studied the genealogy of William Henry Talley. His parents were Horace Alfred Talley of Oak Forest in Cumberland County and Martha Quarles Wills of Chatham in Fluvanna.

Horace was the son of William Peace Talley and Frances Daniel. Married on 25 January 1798, the couple had (according to the husband's will) eight children who survived them: William D., John Archer, Zachariah, Samuel, Edwin P., Joseph H., Martha, and Horace A. Talley. The inventory of the W. P. Talley estate indicated that at the time of his death he owned approximately 600 acres of land, a mill, and fifteen slaves.

Education was apparently very important in this family. The University of Pennsylvania list of Medical Department matriculants shows that during the 1830s Zachariah, William, and Horace Talley received medical degrees from the school. According to the same record Edwin did not graduate, but through the generosity of E. Preston Lancaster, Esq. of Farmville, I now have the medical degree diploma for this brother from the University of Transylvania (University of Kentucky) dated

1835. I also have record that John received his medical degree from the University of Virginia before leaving the state to establish a practice in Missouri. Thus from this family of seven sons, we know that five of them graduated medical school.

Horace Alfred Talley received his degree in 1839, and he married Martha Wills on 7 November 1844. She was the daughter of Dr. John Marshall Wills and his first wife Martha Minor Quarles from Louisa County. The Wills family was then living at Chatham Plantation, where the wedding of young Martha and Horace took place. Chatham is near Rivanna Mills, then a thriving community not far from Columbia.

Before moving to Chatham, John Wills had owned numerous lots and a house in the Town of Columbia where he lived for three years, according to his manservant Burton Payne. This puts the Wills family right on the border of Cumberland County and close enough to the Talleys to provide the close proximity needed to encourage a courtship between Horace and Martha.

The Talleys lived in an area situated along the present Cartersville Road known as Oak Forest several miles north of Cumberland Court House. Information gleaned from a family Bible indicates that William Peace Talley died in 1849 at the home (also called Oak Forest) of his son Horace. This property of 85 acres was not conveyed to the son by deed until 20 September 1852, but by that time he evidently already had possession of it. By 1859 Horace had decided to move or had already moved to Fluvanna and sold Oak Forest to John L. Banks, another Cumberland physician and an in-law of Horace's brother Zachariah. This Zachariah Talley, along with his brothers William and Edwin, remained in Cumberland County and practiced medicine there. The 1865 Confederate Engineer's map of that county identifies the location of three "Doctor Tallys (sic)."

The household of Horace Talley is listed in the 1860 U.S. Census as residents of Fluvanna County at Palmyra Post Office, with real estate valued at $6,500 and personal estate at $18,970. The couple then had three children: William Henry, Eliza M., and Mary L. (Horace and Martha came later.).

By deed dated 15 May 1861, Henry W. and Phebe (sic) A. Wood conveyed to Horace A. Talley, for the sum of $6,500, property described as containing 450 acres, more or less, on the south side of the Rivanna River, adjoining lands of William D. Haden, Jr. (the site of the first Fluvanna courthouse), John B. Omohundro (Pleasure Hill), and Albert Gallatin Wills (Solitude). This is the property surveyed by William S. Clarke, S.F.C. on 15 November 1836, as the 520 acres called LePasture. Some of William Henry's letters in the 1860's are datelined "LePasture," but the place of origin cited on his later letters and those of his father is "Ingleside." It is the same place with different names. In terms of today's landmarks, the Horace Talley homeplace extended from the Rivanna River up Cunningham Creek over a mile, west of where the James Madison Highway crosses the creek, west of Shiloh Church Road past Raccoon Creek, and then back to the river at a point downstream of where this creek enters the river.

It was an exciting but disturbing time in which to live, and Horace surely had some concerns about making so large a commitment. When the delegates to the Virginia Secession Convention had met in February, they voted to remain in the Union but discussions were continued among themselves as well as with the Southern states that had already seceded.

On 15 April 1861 the Richmond papers carried the news that President Lincoln had called for 75,000 troops to put down the "rebellion" and that Virginia would be required to furnish 2,340 of them. The presidential order pushed the delegates to vote for secession rather than furnish troops to fight against other Southern states. The Ordinance of Secession passed on April 17, and the citizens of Virginia ratified it on May 23. When Horace closed on his property the following day, he certainly knew of the convention, but perhaps did not know of the ratification vote.

On the north side of Ingleside was Solitude, the home of Martha Talley's brother, Dr. Albert Gallatin Wills and his family. An apparent surfeit of doctors in the vicinity of the Fluvanna-Cumberland county line had motivated Horace Talley to move to Palmyra. When Wills became a doctor he also moved to Palmyra and set up his practice in a small office in the village beside the stone jail. He first lived in a house (later the site of Old Saints Rest) near Stoneleigh, but in 1860 Wills bought approximately 470 acres of the old Solitude Plantation. This land lay between the Rivanna River and Cunningham Creek, and included the home on a high hill and Solitude Mill located on the creek. Horace Talley and A.G. Wills were not only brothers-in-law and doctors, but also next door neighbors.

Since William Henry was born in December 1847, he was 11 or 12 years old when his family moved to Fluvanna, and he certainly found a neighborhood pal who later gained fame on the national stage. Remember the adjoining landowner on the western boundary of the property Horace purchased? It was John Burwell Omohundro, the father of John Baker Omohundro – who became better known as "Texas Jack." The son was born on 26 July 1846, making him about a year and a half older than William Henry.

Texas Jack Omohundro left home when in his early teens and went to the Lone Star state. He was too young to join the Confederate Army at the outset of the war, but reportedly enlisted in General John Ewell Brown "J.E.B." Stuart's command in 1864, serving as a courier and scout. After the war he returned to Texas and eventually became a good friend and business associate of Buffalo Bill Cody, appearing in the Wild West Show with Cody.*

Perhaps some of Texas Jack's wanderlust rubbed off on his young neighbor, for William Henry would join John Singleton Mosby's Partisan Rangers at an early age. After the war and college, William Henry also caught "Texas Fever," as we shall see.

The Early Years

Unfortunately we know very little about William Henry's childhood and early years, other than the location and a description of his home. Rosa Grant Albert of Richmond, granddaughter of Dr. John and Martha Quarles Wills of Chatham, wrote of many enjoyable summer visits to Fluvanna during the last quarter of the 19th century. Among her favorite relatives was my great grandmother and her great "Aunt Tody," Martha Wills Talley. In *Recollections of Rural Hospitality* (published posthumously in the Fluvanna Historical Society

* For more information see "Texas Jack, The Prairie Whirlwind from Fluvanna County," Fluvanna Historical Society publication #44 (1987).

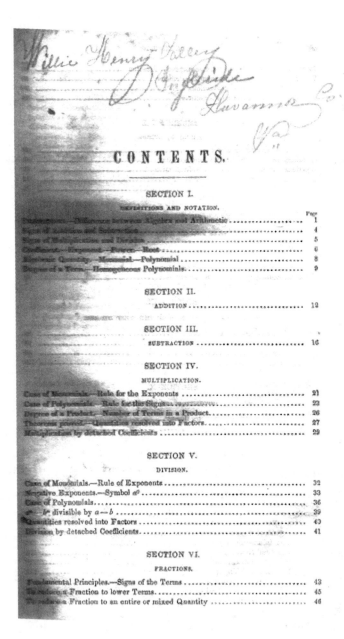

CONTENTS.

Algebra Textbook

18

publication, Number 63-64), she described the Talley home which she inexplicably called "Milton Hill" instead of Ingleside:

It was located on the road between Palmyra and Fork Union, about a mile and a half from Palmyra. Originally the house must have been a three-room structure with two half-story rooms upstairs. Two wings had been added, so that the appearance presented was that of quite a rambling structure.

Rosa went on to say that the house stood a distance back from the road and was surrounded by "a magnificent grove of trees." In season flowers bordered the path from the front gate to the house, and the back yard "sloped gently down to the bank of the Rivanna River."

Thanks to the generosity of a Wills family descendant of Solitude, Roberta Hannah Lloyd, I am in possession of William Henry's Algebra text. This book is something of a story in itself, as it has been used to the point of coming apart, and it carries the names of several owners. The name "Wm. H. Talley" is barely legible on the front cover, but is very plainly written in several places in the first few pages including: "Willie Henry Talley, Ingleside, Fluvanna Co., Va." The book is titled *A Treatise on Algebra* by Elias Loomis, LL.D., published in 1858. The first page has been stamped with a raised seal that reads in part: "T. H. Tutwiler, Attorney at Law & Commissioner in Chancery for Circuit & County Courts of Fluvanna, Palmyra, Fluvanna Co., Va.," and we believe he was an early owner.

In the preface of the book the author states that his earlier edition was "adopted as a text book in half a dozen colleges, besides numerous academies and schools" and suggests that a student fifteen years old of average ability should not be discouraged by the text. I have reviewed some of it and can assure you that it is a difficult algebra book, but perhaps more was expected of students at that time. All evidence proves William Henry used this book in the equivalent of our present-day high school rather than in college. That he used his home address further supports this. So judging by this book, wherever he received his early schooling, I feel confident that it was a good education.

Mosby Ranger

When the Civil War began in 1861, William Henry was 13 years of age, too young to serve in any unit, and he was not old enough before the end of the war to be subject to the draft. However, he volunteered for service with Mosby's Rangers (43rd Battalion, Virginia Cavalry) and enlisted as a private in Company D, formed on 28 March 1864. Mosby's exploits have lived beyond him and become legend, even inspiring a television series, "The Gray Ghost."

Mosby is the most noted officer of the Confederacy whose family lived in Fluvanna. His father Alfred Mosby owned the home we know as Cumber between March 1854 and December 1862. There his sisters had so many dances that the home was soon called "Dancing Hall." It is said that on one occasion when their brother was home, he took a diamond ring and carved his initials on a window pane in the schoolhouse in the yard. That window is long gone, but the story survives.

Mosby had served without particular distinction in several units before being noticed by General J.E.B. Stuart who came to like and trust him, and became something of a mentor to him. Mosby proposed that he be allowed to operate as a partisan and conduct a guerrilla operation behind Yankee lines to harass the enemy and interrupt its communications and supply lines.

The Partisan Ranger Law provided that when partisans turned over captured military equipment to the quartermaster, they could keep non-military items. Each man could decide whether to keep or sell what he had received. The whole partisan ranger scenario was very much like the earlier commissions that governments gave to privateers allowing them to attack vessels of the enemy and keep any ships and other spoils they could capture. Mosby's men proved very effective for the Confederacy and for themselves. From the "Greenback Raid" for example, when they captured a Federal payroll of $172,000, each participant received more than $2,000. We should note that Mosby always refused any share of the spoils.

Before the war ended the Confederacy decided to revoke most of the partisan ranger commissions, but General Lee recommended that Mosby's men and another unit be allowed to continue without change. Apparently by that time Lee had gained respect for the military discipline Mosby maintained over his command as well as the effectiveness of his operations.

Mosby's tactics made the enemy support his operations – especially with the fast horses his rangers captured. Mosby's men were often outnumbered, and good horses were the key to escape. Rangers were responsible for furnishing their own horses and weapons, so essentially they cost the Confederacy little, while they furnished Lee's army with captured materials.

Mosby said in his *Memoirs*:

> We drew nothing from Richmond except the gray jackets my men wore. We were mounted, armed and equipped entirely off the enemy, but as we captured a great deal more than we could use, the surplus was sent to supply Lee's army.

Mosby had realized from the beginning that the primary benefit of this type of action would force the Union to tie up so many of its troops to guard the railroads, telegraph lines, wagon trains, and other infrastructure necessary to support its army. This kept thousands of Yankee troops from the front lines against the Army of Virginia.

While we do not know in which raids or actions William Henry participated, he evidently stayed with the Rangers until the end of the war. Mosby did not surrender his command as a unit after Lee surrendered but conducted a final roll call and told his men, "I disband your organization in preference to surrendering to our enemies." This left each man to seek his own parole. (Mosby was initially denied parole and did not receive his papers for almost a year and then only after Union General Ulysses S. Grant intervened on his behalf.)

William Henry Talley was paroled at Columbia, Virginia in May 1865. We do not know the exact date, as the Union officer in command, Major Henry Terwilliger of New York, did not date the parole papers of any individual. William Henry was erroneously listed as serving in Company L, but a review of the original papers reveals that the "D" was partially smeared and was mistakenly transcribed as an "L."

In retrospect William Henry probably joined the Rangers for the same reasons many others did. It was possible for him to enlist at a young age. Mosby preferred young recruits, perhaps thinking the brashness of youth and a lack of regard for their own mortality made them better suited for the venture. Further, it was the view of most Virginians that their state had been invaded, and there was a strong patriotic fervor to repel the Northern aggression. The newspapers had reported on the exploits of Mosby, and when William Henry became a Ranger in 1864, less than a year after the Battle of Gettysburg, it must have seemed to him that Mosby was the only Southern force on the offensive meeting with some success. Additionally, the promise of adventure and the possibility of captured rewards may have motivated him to join.

Back to School

William Henry returned to Fluvanna to receive his parole after the war, and then went home to Ingleside. He undoubtedly fell behind in his education while with Mosby, and he now resumed his schooling.

He was a contemporary and lifelong friend of James Osgood Shepherd (later Judge J. O. Shepherd) of Mountain View at Palmyra, and in the years after the war when either traveled, their correspondence provided the other, and now us, with news of Fluvanna. We print here one of the letters James received when he taught school at Bent Creek in Appomattox County. It is full of news of mutual friends, refers to charming ladies, and Talley's final exams. He is now "out of school." The letter is surprisingly light-hearted considering that the days after the war were very hard for many. William Henry was eighteen at the time of this letter.

Lepasture, April 17, 1866

Dear James,

Although I am very slow in answering your letter, yet trusting a little to your leniency, knowing that plausibility of my many excuses, which are too numerous to mention, will be admitted; and acting upon the old maxim of "better late than never"; will attempt to write a few lines; and only a few, as it is getting late, and I am tired after having worked hard all day at the carpenter's trade. In the meantime Pete (Abram Shepherd III) came over to see me desiring me to accompany him to Appoma(ttox) to see you which I would have been delighted to do but circumstances would not admit.

I was at the University on the 13th at the celebration of the Jefferson Society, had a very nice time but would have had a still nicer had I been lucky enough to have been acquainted with some of the numerous fair ones who were present on the occasion. We had a very eloquent speech delivered to us in the hall, which was magnificently decorated and illuminated; after which the ladies and gentlemen promenaded on the beautifully illuminated lawn, feasting on love and music, for in the centre of the lawn a band from Richmond was stationed, whose music echoed and reechoed through the surrounding country, completing the celebrity of the occasion. But I will ____ school of renown and speak of one still more so: Whortleberry Academy which has to my sad regret no more charms for me.* Mr. Abell closed with an examination of four days ending the 29th March, during which time (we) were

---

* Without any record of a Fluvanna school with this name, the identification was perhaps fictitious and used to amuse his friend.

honored with the presence of ladies every day, with whom I enjoyed myself talking to them on every occasion except when being examined from which cause I had to study nearly all night in reviewing the studies on which I were to be examined the next day, but the examination is over and to my credit I came out perfect in all my studies.

I am out of a school now and nothing to do but to work and try to study at home which I find is very hard to do. Do you know where I can get a school up in your part of the country, something after your own? Mr. Abell advised me to get one if I could, that it would be just as improving as going to school for a while. I do not like the idea much, but if I do have to leave home I would rather be near you if I could. Inquire around and see if there is any chance for me, but what ever you do, keep it a secret, do not let anyone know that I have this idea unless some one wishes to employ me, then you can give them my address.

I had a nice time last Easter, went fishing with some ladies but caught no fish except some on land. It is reported that Miss Mary Sue Thomas is to be married soon to Rily Toney. Miss Dollie requested me to inform you that she had not forgotten that Tilapoena present. Miss Maggie has left us as her time was out but left it as a standing message to give her love to you. Bev & Henry spend a good portion of their time at Capt. Clarke's. Nothing else to write so I must close as I reckon it is time for all working men to be in bed. Answer this immediately and I will be prompt in returning an answer. Could write several sheets, but have not the time, answer this, do not treat me as I have done you. "Return good for evil." All join me in love to you.

Wm. H. Talley

Cadet W. H. Talley
VMI - Class of 1870

College Student

We do not know if William Henry taught school before he decided to enroll at the Virginia Military Institute (VMI) in Lexington. His letter to the school's superintendent accepting his appointment follows:

> *Palmyra, Fluvanna, Va.*
> *Aug. 18th, 1867*

Gen. F. H. Smith

General,

> *I received an appointment as Cadet in the Virginia Military Institute by last mail, and hasten to inform you of my acceptance. It is impossible for me to report by the 20th as I have some preparations to make before I can leave, but will report as soon as possible.*
>
> *Respectfully,*
> *W. H. Talley*

Archival records at VMI indicate that he reported for duty on August 27. We can imagine that he used the week before that to raise some money for tuition, as apparently finances were stretched thin in the family. William Henry entered as a "pay cadet" who had to cover his own tuition, room, and board. He had apparently applied for entry as a "state cadet" whose fees were paid as a scholarship by the Commonwealth of Virginia, but he was not selected. By the end of his first year, the family's financial situation had deteriorated even more, and he again sought to be made a "state cadet."

John Letcher was Governor of Virginia from 1860 to 1864, and after the end of his term he had returned home to Lexington to practice law. He was a member of the VMI Board of Visitors from 1866 until 1880, and served as president of the board for ten years. It was in this capacity that his brother-in-law, John Chapman Blackwell, solicited him on behalf of William Henry Talley. William Henry likely knew the Blackwell family before the war when J.C. Blackwell was president of Buckingham Female Institute, located just south of the James River and the Fluvanna-Buckingham county line. Several young women of Fluvanna, including the Shepherds of Mountain View and the Woods of Spring Garden, attended the institute – the "first woman's college in Virginia."

R(andolph) M(acon) College, May 28th, 1868

Governor,

You have, no doubt, forgotten that I once—two years ago I think—recommended to you a young gentleman of Fluvanna, Mr. Wm. H. Talley for the place of State Cadet in the Va. M. Institute from his District. He then failed to get the place, because it had been promised to a young man, already in the institution as a pay Cadet, whenever a vacancy should occur. That young man will graduate in July next. Now, this is to request your influence in favor of the same Mr. Talley, who is now a pay Cadet in the Institute. He will be unable to remain longer than July, unless he can get the place. His father lost much of his property by the war, & much also in the way of bankrupt notices. I think your kindness—from all I learn of this young gentleman, and this chiefly from my son John—could not be shown to any person who promises more of usefulness

than Mr. Talley.
We are all pretty well ....

In much love,
Jno. C. Blackwell

The lack of any response from VMI prompted Horace Talley to ask for an answer for his son.

Palmyra, Va. Oct 10th
Gov. Letcher.
Dear Sir,
Mr. Blackwell addressed you a short time since recommending my son, Wm. H. Talley, as State Cadet in place of his son, who rec'd the appointment but had declined its acceptance. As I have heard nothing relative to that recommendation, you will please write me at Palmyra informing me what action, if any, the board has taken in the matter, and much obliged,
Yours respectfully,
H. A. Talley

We do not know if Horace Talley ever got a response to his letter. Regardless, William Henry remained at the school.

VMI records show that William Henry Talley graduated on 4 July 1870, with a class rank of 33rd out of 52 cadets. His ranking in each course taken is also given, and it appears that his best subjects were chemistry, Latin, French, English studies and literature, and military engineering. His war service had prepared him for the rigorous discipline of VMI, for he was one of only three cadets in his class that received absolutely no demerits during his years there. By comparison, two of his classmates received over 700 demerits during the same time. At his graduation, in addition to his diploma and *Societe d' Cadets* certificate signed by all of his classmates, he was given a Bible that he treasured the rest of his life.

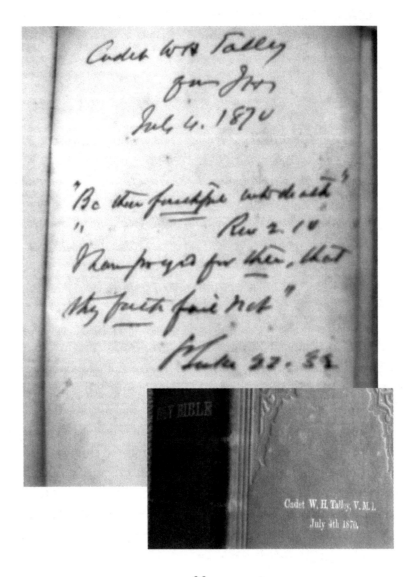

Teacher and Administrator

After graduation from VMI, William Henry again returned home to Ingleside and began his teaching career. Among the archives of the Fluvanna Historical Society, we found a report and roll book from 28 February 1871, kept by "William Henry Talley, a teacher in the Fluvanna public schools." He reported having 18 male and 8 female pupils, and among these students was his younger brother, Horace. On the back of the report, our teacher noted that the school

> is situated about 3 ¼ miles from Palmyra immediately on the C. H. road in a tolerably comfortable house, has two [illegible]… to the fuel is very convenient. I am authorized by the Bd. of Trustees to give two Dollars per month for house & wood but have made arrangements to have the wood cut so that the scholars have nothing to do but put it on the fire.

William Henry did not remain in Fluvanna more than a year, as the Briscoe Center for American History of the University of Texas at Austin has among its collections a letter written by him on 24 February 1872, when he was Commandant of Cadets at Goldsboro Military Institute in North Carolina. The letter was addressed to his cousin Fleming Wills James, then affiliated with Texas Military Institute (TMI) at Austin.

Dear Flem,
Your most welcome and interesting letter came to hand several days since and … I am glad to know all are getting on so well, hope you may succeed in Law equally as well.

Our school is in its infancy. We have only 23 at present—but are daily expecting more. There were only 8 when I arrived here. But I doubt whether we can succeed in building up much of a Military School here for there are too many in this state already. You wished to know my rank. I am second in command & as we have only one company I reckon I rank as Captain. I am comd of cadets, Profes of Math & higher English and Geography. I have my hands full. I am busy about six hours a day. I only get my board and $40.00 per month. Don't expect to remain if my salary is not raised after this term. Profes offers to make me an equal partner with himself. But I don't like to run any risks. I want some sure pay. ... I don't like this section of the country. It is too low and marshy. I may stay but I have an idea of going to the V.M. I. next session and taking a Special course.

I received a letter from Father today. He said that it has been one of the hardest winters he ever saw. All were well at home & Aunt Mat's. Farmers are very much behind here & in VA. Most of the hands have gone to the R. Road & some have not hired, many others have only a few. Don't you wish you could have enjoyed the fine scating [sic] that they have had in Va this winter; for three weeks the river was frozen in some places 10 inches thick....

William Henry remained at Goldsboro for only one or two years and then returned to Fluvanna. His obituary stated that he also taught at a military school in Louisiana, but we have not been able to confirm his employment there. However, the TMI newspaper, *The Texas Cadet*, in its November 1875 issue lists Capt. W. H. Talley as Instructor in Mathematics and

BATTALION ORGANIZATION

OF THE

CORPS CADETS.

Colonel F. W. James,.. Commandant Cadets
Capt. W. H. Talley.... Assistant Com. Cadets

CADET OFFICERS.

"A" COMPANY.

Captain.................................L. K. Rose
First Lieutenant...............C. O. Barton
First Sergeant...........W. von Rosenberg
Sergeant.............................J. R. Raby
Sergeant..............................W. Moore
Corporal...............................R. Moore
Corporal..........................J. E. Burford

"B" COMPANY.

Captain............................J. E. Binkley
First Lieutenant..................A. T. Rose
First Sergeant...................R. P. Smyth
Sergeant.............................F. Holman
Sergeant..........................J. L. Shepherd
Corporal..........................P. M. Bowie
Corporal...........................P. A. Rogan

"C" COMPANY.

Captain............................A. E. Rector
First Lieutenant.......................J. Coke
First Sergeant................C. H. Earnest
Sergeant.........................J. W. Phillips
Sergeant............................J. D. Brown
Sargeant........................A. S. Johnson
Corporal........................E. McDannell
Corporal.........................C. M. Bunton
Corporal..........................R. Kuechler

COLOR GUARD.

Color Sergeant ....T. E. Littlefield
Corporal...........................L. W. Rector
Corporal...........................H. C. Brown
Corporal...........................H. B. Wilson

STAFF.

Adjutant..............................J. A. Baker
Serjeant Major.......................J. Horner
Quartermaster Sergeant ....A. Wills

Drum Major.......................J. R. Fisk

HENKELS.

TEXAS MILITARY INSTITUTE.

AUSTIN, TEXAS.

ACADEMIC STAFF.

Col. John G. James, Professor Mathematics.

Col. Fleming W. James, Professor Military Tactics and Engineering.

Maj. H. H. Dinwiddie, Professor Physics and Chemistry.

Maj. W. L. Bringhurst, Professor of Ancient Languages.

Capt. W. H. Talley, Instructor in Mathematics and English Studies.

Col. John G. James, Acting Professor Modern Languages, History and Literature.

Prof. Wm. Besserer, Professor of Music.

MILITARY STAFF.

Col. John G. James, Superintendent.
Col. F. W. James, Commandant of Cadets.
Dr. J. B. Shepherd, Surgeon.

The Texas Cadet
November 1875

English Studies, and in the "Battalion Organization of the Corps Cadets" he is listed as Assistant Commandant of Cadets, after Col. Fleming W. James, Commandant of Cadets. The cousins had maintained contact, and William Henry had gone to Texas to teach with Fleming and his brother John Garland James.

The James men were sons of Henry James and his wife Eliza Maria Wills, William Henry's maternal aunt. Besides being Talley cousins, the brothers were also graduates of VMI. There John had finished with second honors in the Class of 1866, and Fleming was valedictorian in 1868 – the year John was president of TMI. Another brother Charles taught at TMI but died in 1875. An alumnus of Fluvanna Military Institute and the University of Virginia, he helped in 1861 form the Fluvanna Hornets, Company F, 44th Virginia Infantry. In 1879 (after William Henry had left), TMI became a part of the Agricultural and Mechanical College of Texas with John James as its new president, and he is recognized as having been the second president of what is now Texas A&M University. John was forever a proud Virginian, and the inscription on his Austin, Texas grave stone included "Born in Chatham Fluvanna Co. Va."

William Henry had remained at TMI for the 1875-1876 session and then moved to another military school, as *The Texas Cadet* in September 1876 stated: "Capt. W. H. Talley, formerly assistant professor of mathematics in this Institute, is now occupying a place in Coronal Institute, San Marcos. He is an affable gentleman, and will do well." I have been unable to find records from this Methodist school to confirm how long he was there. However, after the death of their father, both William Henry and his younger brother Horace gave depositions that provide some details of the older brother's career.

35

From these statements, the timeline of William Henry's activities for most of the decade after his graduation from VMI would be:

Fall 1870-Spring 1871: farming and teaching in
Fluvanna
Fall 1871-Spring 1872: teaching at Goldsboro Military
Institute
Summer 1872-Spring 1873: probably at Goldsboro,
but possibly in Louisiana
Summer 1873-Fall 1875: back home in Fluvanna
farming
Fall 1875-Spring 1876: teaching at Texas Military
Institute
Fall 1876-Spring 1878: teaching at Coronal Institute

Possibly William Henry found the salary that he earned from teaching inadequate for his needs, because he used so much of it to support his family in Fluvanna. His father often wrote him asking for help. One letter reads in part: "Ingleside, March 28th, '73, Dear Willie, I received yours on last night containing a check for seventy five dollars for which I am very much obliged; as it seems almost impossible to make any collections here."

William Henry paid much of the tuition to put his sister Mary through Hollins Institute (Hollins University). We have a 26 September 1873 receipt for $100 and one dated 20 May 1874 for $28.73, both on account of board and tuition at Hollins for Mary. The next decade, we know from his daybook, William Henry paid his brother Horace's tuition at University College of Medicine (Medical College of Virginia).

These amounts may seem inconsequential, but when you consider that William Henry was earning $40 per month while teaching in North Carolina, with a school year of no more than eight months, we can see that he sent over $200, or more than five months' salary, to support his family. He probably sent other amounts that are not documented.

Although his father continued to farm and practice medicine, it seems that his finances continued to worsen, and he sought and received ever more assistance from his son. By letter in March 1877, Horace Talley writes:

> *Dear Willie, as your Mama has written you all the news of the neighborhood, I will simply write a few lines on business. Last spring I bought $84.00 worth of Guano, payment of which becomes due 1ˢᵗ April. Failing to make a crop of tobacco I will not be able to meet it. If you can send me that amount you will very much oblige ....Send it if you can without too much inconvenience to yourself.*
> *Your devoted father,*
> *H. A. Talley*

Apparently, William Henry was able to send a check for the full amount as his father wrote him in April thanking him and advising his son not to return home to Fluvanna due to the economic problems in the area:

> *Palmyra, April 18ᵗʰ, '77*
>
> *Dear Willie,*
> *I reckon you have been expecting a letter from me but I have been so busy professionally & on the farm as to prevent me from writing until now.*

I received the check in yours to your Mama, for which I return many thanks, for I assure you it is almost as scarce here as hen's teeth. All of the banks & Insurance companies in Charlottesville have gone up & a good many of the people of Albemarle with them, several of the Professors will have to go into bankruptcy...

I am getting on very well with my farming operation, nearly ready to commence planting corn but will not plant any until about 1ˢᵗ of May. Tobacco plants in abundance at this time, but very small, it is full early for them, however my wheat is looking finely, my lot is said by everybody that has seen it to be the best in the county.

You seem to be very much dissatisfied with your location but if you will take my advice you will remain where you are if you can make $10.00 per month as that is more than you can make here. I would like very much to see you and would be happy to have you with me all the time, but times are such here at this time as to force me to advise you to stay where you are for one more year at least, as it is impossible for you to do anything here.

Times in this county are worse then the oldest inhabitants ever witnessed, not one man in twenty has corn enough.

We had a Tableaux at Bethel [Church] last Saturday, owing to the day being so cold and disagreeable the attendance was small, we however made $60.00. Tomorrow night the Methodists will have one in Palmyra.

I believe I have given you all the news in general. Eliza will write you in a few days and give all the particulars. We are all well at home & your Aunt Mat.

Your devoted father, H. A. Talley

The hard economic times that Horace describes in this and subsequent letters were symptomatic of the "Panic of 1873" that gripped the country at least until 1878. As Robert McNamara said in "Financial Panics of the 19th Century" at About.com:

> The stock market dropped sharply and caused numerous businesses to fail. The depression caused approximately three million Americans to lose their jobs. The collapse in food prices impacted America's farm economy, causing great poverty in rural America.

These are exactly the effects that Horace described in his letters. Unfortunately, it appears that the fortunes of the family did not rebound when the depression supposedly ended in 1878.

Family Obligations

William Henry returned home from Texas a month before his father died in August 1878, and as the administrator of Horace's estate he undertook to save his mother and siblings from the poorhouse as creditors pressed their claims. A creditor's suit was filed to subject the assets to payment of all bills before any distribution to the heirs, and a public announcement of this action appeared over a year after Horace's death in the legal notices section of the 29 November 1879 issue of the *Richmond Whig.* The plaintiffs were listed as: Perkins & Haden, Allison & Addison, James O. Shepherd Administrator of R.C. Strange, Harris and Shepherd, Jr. doing business, suing on behalf of themselves, and "all other creditors of H.A. Talley, deceased, who may come in and contribute their due proportion to the costs of this suit."

Defendants in the suit were the deceased's immediate family: "Wm. H. Talley in his own right, and as administrator of H.A. Talley, deceased; Martha Q. Talley, widow of said H.A. Talley; [and his four other children] Eliza M. Shepherd, Mary L. Talley, Horace Talley, and Martha Talley, the last two being infants, under 21 years of age."

The normal procedure in a suit of this nature is for the Court to refer it to a Commissioner in Chancery, who puts a notice of the lawsuit in the newspaper and advises all interested parties of the date and place for taking claims against the estate. Then the Commissioner reviews the accounts of the Administrator of the estate, determines which creditors have claims and in what amounts, and what assets are in the estate to pay those claims. Then enough property is sold to pay the claims and what is left is distributed to the heirs. This may be something of an oversimplification of any process involving multiple lawyers, but that is basically what should take place. Also, the Court has an obligation to protect the interests of the minor children who are parties to the suit, so the Commissioner would evaluate the bill of each creditor and see how much to allow.

In this case there were a number of other factors to complicate the process. Due to the lack of cash in the economy at that time, it was common practice for people to give each other notes or due bills to evidence debts, and then pay these by barter, exchange of goods or labor. For example, attorney A. A. Gray filed a claim against the estate for $10 plus $20 for representation in various legal matters. Then he offset $27 against his $30 bill, as this was the amount he owed Horace Talley for medical services, which would have left a $3.00 balance. However, Mr. Gray claimed interest due on his account of an additional $3.00 (a rather stiff 10% of his bill), but he did not compute any offsetting interest due on the medical bill.

Commissioner J.J. Powell undertook to settle these accounts, and made his report to the Court. It should have presented no problem as the estate was due much more than it owed. However, the doctor was too generous in furnishing medical care to people who needed it but had little ability to pay. The Commissioner reported that nearly 300 persons owed money to the estate, most of these small amounts of $1.00 to $5.00, with a few as much as $50 on open account, and he was owed $661.60 evidenced by bonds and due bills payable to his estate. However, out of the total of $4,537 owed to the estate, the Commissioner reported that he expected only $581.50 likely would ever be collected, and he considered the balance "doubtful or worthless." In addition, the Commissioner found other personal property valued at $1,166, and 454 acres of real estate valued at $6.00 per acre, or $2,724 total (subject to the dower interest of his widow) would be available to pay debts. (This is the same property that Horace had purchased less than 20 years earlier for $6500 at over $14 an acre.)

The Commissioner reported that the estate had debts that totaled $2,282.54, plus interest of $758.06, for a combined $3,040.60. If we use the Commissioner's figures for assets of $581.50 of debt that could be collected, plus $1,166 of personal property that could be sold, and real estate valued at $2,724, we have a total of $4,471.50 that would be available to pay creditors, leaving $1,430.90 available for the family. It was very simple in theory, but not so simple in practice.

The first complication was the dower interest of the widow, Martha Talley. Dower (not dowry) was part of the common law we inherited from England. Married women did not own property. Any property that a woman brought into the marriage became her husband's, who could dispose of it as he saw fit. However, allowing unscrupulous or uncaring husbands to leave their wives destitute and a burden on the community seemed bad policy, so the concept of dower came into the law. A widow has the right to the use and income from one-third of the real property that her husband owned during the marriage. In this case, assuming all the land had equal value, Martha was entitled to the use of 151 acres. The Court appointed four commissioners – J. Haden Martin, C. O. Perkins, J. P. White, and J. E. Desper – to engage a surveyor to determine the dower interest of the widow. The commissioners reported on 30 March 1880 stating that the metes and bounds of the dower interest were shown by the survey plat accompanying the report.

Unfortunately, no plat can be found among the suit papers or in the land records of Fluvanna County, so we cannot tell what part of the land was set aside for her. However, we know that Martha's dower claim ended with her death. I have not been able to determine the date of her death, but although in bad health she was alive in 1903. By deed dated 16 July 1906, her dower tract was conveyed to W. P. Haden, so we know she had died by then.

No one wants to lose his homeplace, and William Henry felt it was his duty to protect his mother and siblings and keep them in the home they knew. He undertook to operate the farm, keeping the family there, and doing everything he legally could to prevent any sale of the property. It seems he manipulated the legal system with some success, much to the chagrin of the commissioners, who only get their fee from the sale price.

By report dated 11 November 1886, one of the commissioners appointed by the court to sell several lots of land complained that he could not complete a public auction of this property and requested that he be allowed to sell it privately. His reason was that he had been authorized to resell three lots of the land by decree in November 1885, and had advertised and held auction sales of the land on court days in December and the following year in February, April, June, August, and October. However, he had been unsuccessful because "At every offering almost the former purchaser William H. Talley runs the land up and has it knocked out to him, and then invariable (sic) fails to comply with the purchase." This is actually a very clever tactic, as it insures the property will be sold for the top price, and in this case it prevented any sale. The frustrated commissioner could have advertised that if the successful bidder failed to complete the purchase the property would be offered to the backup bidder at his high bid, but that was apparently not done.

William Henry managed to stall these sales for years, and in the Fluvanna County Clerk's Office are deeds that record the eventual resolution of his father's lands. However, it took over 25 years:

- 25 December 1883 [Christmas Day?] – 21 acres to Harrison Hughson for $126
- 25 May 1888 – 52 ½ acres to Eliza (Shepherd) Page (sister of William Henry) for $479
- 29 June 1893 – 71 ¼ acres and 87 ¼ acres to Eliza Page for $135.24.
- 16 July 1906 – 55 acres for $305 and the Dower Tract of 160 acres for $500, both to W. P. Haden
- 20 February 1909 – 22 acres to Wallace W. Wills (cousin of William Henry) for $62

W. H. Talley

The suit filed in 1879 against the Talley Estate had already been long and arduous, and it was not yet finished.

The Daybook

Now, let's talk about the daybook that covers part of 1882 and 1883. The original questions about it were: "Who kept it?" and "Why was it found at Mountain View, the home of J.O. Shepherd?"

William Henry, like many farmers of his day, kept records of his day-to-day activities, noting how much fertilizer and seed he used in which fields, and what yield was produced and the weather conditions or how much feed his animals required and which cows had calves, for example, as this sort of information would help him make decisions about what practices are efficient and productive. This daybook provides neither the beginning nor the end of the story, but a section from the middle of a detailed narrative of farm life and activities.

Since the court took the position in the suit against the Horace Talley Estate that the creditors were entitled to any profits from the farm operation, my guess is that William Henry used this record as the basis for some of the testimony he would give regarding his father's estate. J.O. Shepherd was the attorney for one of the creditors, had the right to review the notes that a witness uses in his testimony, and may have done so and then gotten the daybook mixed up with his own documents.

It is worth noting that while the parties and attorneys to this lawsuit were on opposite sides of the legal issues, they seemed to remain on a very friendly basis. A. A. Gray was an attorney in Palmyra who had represented Horace Talley, and he continued to represent William Henry. There are numerous references in the daybook to transactions with Gray, and many visits and even overnight stays at his house Clifton (now known as Thomas Hill across U.S. 15 from Mountain View) by the Talley family. In the daybook William Henry mentions having dinner at J. J. Powell's residence when traveling home from Richmond. He was the commissioner in chancery first appointed to take accountings in the case. William Henry also remained close to J.O. Shepherd, who was later a member of his friend's wedding party.

The portion of the daybook that we have covers approximately five months, with a pretty detailed account of each day's activities. He keeps track of which family members are at home, and who visits at their home. Two young men named Peter and Robert lived on the place and helped with the farm work. Usually payment was worked out by an exchange of labor or farm produce instead of money.

At this time William Henry was paying the tuition for his younger brother Horace to attend medical school in Richmond, and he occasionally visited him. This involved traveling to Columbia by horseback or buggy and taking the train to Richmond (fare of $3.85). Once in the capital city he enjoyed taking walks, and we found he had a weakness for oysters and cigars. However, he never failed to purchase gifts to bring back to his family.

I will quote a couple of representative days, and then select a few passages that may be interesting for their view of events in Fluvanna at that time. Any information in brackets is my explanation and not part of the original daybook.

Oct. 18th—Peter harrowed clover lot for wheat with Jack & Redeye [a mule and a horse respectively]. Carter helped me an hour to clean wheat then went home. Robert & I shucked, pulled & cleaned up some corn. Ben Tyree had cart & oxen to haul a load of corn. Jno. Woodson paid me a flour barrel of corn. Jno. Wilkinson worked for me from after breakfast until 10 ½ o'clock, carried a load planks from mill to A. A. Gray's—Albert Jones hauled 2 loads corn to my barn for Ben Woodson, nearly 7 barrels (according to their measure 6 5/6 barrels). He carried one barrel home for hauling Ben's [share] there. Warm & clear. A. A. Gray one load planks, .75c.

Oct. 19*th*—Peter, Robert & I worked on corn until dinner hauling into cornhouse & shucking etc. Peter harrowed on clover lot in evening. Robert shucked corn. I went to James P. Noel's to buy a young ox & called by Post office. Mailed a letter to Ashby James. Furnished stamp for Mother. I paid .11c for Farmers Friend [brand of plow] point at Tutwiler's—Mattie rode Mary to school. She was taken very lame in her swelled leg. Rained gradually nearly all day. Mother received a postal from Eliza & a letter from Horace.

Oct. 20*th*—Robert & I fallowed [plowed but left unseeded] some with oxen. Peter fallowed & harrowed with horses on the piece of land that was left out in clover lot. Lewis Anderson brought ten bu. & 8 lbs. wheat to mill for me, exchanged it for some seed wheat with me. Jno. Wilkinson shucked out what corn he had hauled up—4 flour barrels good & 2 nubbings [few grains on cob]. I went with Peter, Robert, Will, Clay & Jno. W. opossum hunting. We hunted until 1 o'clock, caught 2 small opossums—Jno. W. cut his sorghum this evening.

Oct. 21*st*—1882, Saturday. Jno. W. hauled up 2 loads lowground corn with my oxen & his in front of them. Peter fallowed awhile then harrowed, finished clover lot—I cut corn, finished the piece back of corn house, fallowed in some peas, gathered some, hauled up 2 loads guano from lowgrounds, worked Maggie in front of oxen [to keep oxen in line] with one load, Jack the other. Charlie Bethel brought the guano up from Columbia & put it off on my lowgrounds. [I believe he operated a batteau and brought the guano up the Rivanna from Columbia.] I paid him $2.00 cash on it. Peter & Robert hauled up 2 loads of the corn I cut down. I went to Palmyra in evening for the mail. Cool & cloudy.

Oct. 22nd, Sunday. I went to Cunningham Church. Mr. Wray preached, I took dinner at J. E. Desper's. [Interesting that none of the family went with him.] Cool & cloudy most of day—Jeff came over this morning to see how the well was getting on.

Oct. 23rd, Monday, Court Day. I paid $7.00 to Jeff for mother for fixing the well. [Illegible] an order for a barrel of flour, $6.00 & 2 gals molasses, also paid James P. Noel $12.00 for a young ox to be delivered to me on or before the day of his Father's sale. I also gave Jacob Fontaine .10c, he being sick and unable to work. I sowed about ¾ bushel oats before breakfast, after breakfast hauled up corn & tops [saved top of corn stalk] off lot back of corn house. Threw out corn stubbles & cultivated rows down. Went to court and rode over woods with A. J. Taylor to look at timber. Peter & Robert helped about corn & harrowed oats on lowgrounds & pulled some corn off—I wrote a postal to Ben Woodson about buying his corn. E. E. Tutwiler paid me $15.00 on a/c wheat sold him but not delivered—rained nearly all night. Jno. Wilkinson hauled his sorghum to Haden's.

The narrative continues on in similar fashion for the next five months. More highlights:

Nov. 7ᵗʰ, 1882, Election Day. Massie & Odersel, Democratic Candidates for Congress at large & 7ᵗʰ dist—received 23 votes at Jones school house [near Central Elementary School]. Jno. S. Wise & Jno. Paul for same offices on Republican ticket, 49 each. For Constitutional Amendments—50; against, 22 votes—There was more fraud used in this election than in any election since the war (in my opinion). Peter helped Ben Tyree sow wheat & oats—sowed a bu of each & plowed in some oats that were sowed yesterday. Warmer today and cloudy—Christopher Harlan had Maggie to ride to Election. I acted as Judge of the election today at Jones' schoolhouse—Ben Tyree got 1 bu wheat & 1 bu oats today."

The next day, he notes "Democratic victory in County yesterday, 55 majority." In December William Henry celebrated his 35ᵗʰ birthday by working as usual; at this time he was storing ice:

Dec. 19ᵗʰ. My birthday, spent it hard at work, getting ice, etc. Peter, Stuart & I hauled 11 loads. Robert threw the ice in ice house. Miles cut wood at woodpile from 10 o'clock until night. We hauled [ice] with oxen & Jack. I have now put in 24 loads. Peter's Grandmother came over and I paid her part of Peter's hire up to January 10ᵗʰ, 1883. Viz $2.25 cash, 1 gal molasses, 6 ½ lbs flour & 10 lbs salt pork—in all $4.25—Maggie improving slowly. I mended one of Martha's shoes last night. Sent a flour barrel to mill to put Jeff's flour in for fixing the well—I pulled out 8 loads ice by myself today besides cutting it and helping to load & threw some in ice house. Weather moderated some.

Dec. 25*th*, Christmas day, Mother, Mollie, Mattie & I went to Bethel to Oyster dinner. Horace went to Courthouse. I spent 50c. paid Horace $2.00 for making suit of clothes I got of him. Peter, Robert, Stuart & Jeter spent 75c at Clifton's in Christmas tricks. Harrison Hughson came here for balance due him on Monroe a/c $8.50—I borrowed $3.50 of H. to pay him—Mrs. Haden & Partheus sat until bedtime. Robert's father came spent the night.

January 1*st*, 1883. I attended auction at Tutwiler's [Stoneleigh] day and until 11 o'clock at night—bought good many articles—I worked all the time handing things & putting them away. Peter went hunting.

January 2*nd*, Mother & I went to spend the day—a dining day at A. A. Gray's. Mother spent the night. We had a magnificent dinner. Peter carried some Bacon to Palmyra to be shipped to A. L. Shepherd of Richmond, 27 lbs middling, then cut about 3 arms full of wood was all he did complaining of sore throat.

William Henry was willing to help his neighbors in time of need. He recounts several instances of offering to sit up with sick neighbors or with the remains of the deceased.

Jan. 28*th*, Sunday, I came by Dr. Perkin's to see Henry. Took dinner at John Adams' then went to Dr. P.'s, sat up all night with Henry, who died at 3 ½ o'clock A. M. Ely Tutwiler, J. Adams, Henry Saddler & I shrouded him. There

*was no one in the room when he died except Dr. P., J. A.,
and I. He died very easily and was perfectly willing to die.
Only dreaded strangling—rained in evening and at night.*

The Ongoing Suit and Another Complication

We earlier calculated that the creditors' suit against the
estate of Horace Talley had an active life of thirty years. Its legal
life was considerably longer. Even after the last parcel of land
was sold in 1909, none of the parties showed any interest in
ending the suit. No action was taken and no orders entered
until it was ended by the court in 1926. This means that the
case was on the court docket from 1879 to 1926, for a total
lifespan of forty-seven years, outliving many of the parties
including William Henry.

As if the Horace Talley creditors' suit had not become
complicated enough, for some reason the parties to that matter
agreed to combine their suit with the one involving the Solitude
estate of Dr. Albert Gallatin Wills (Horace's brother-in-law). A
creditor named Leftwich had obtained a judgment against Wills
in 1861 that had not been paid, and after Wills's death in 1870,
other creditors surfaced. However, the doctor specified in his
will that the bulk of his estate should be kept together for the
use of his wife and until their children had all come of age. The
parties were apparently trying to respect his wishes and settle
the debts from income rather than selling the property. The
chief income producing asset of the estate was the Solitude mill.
At one time this was rented for $500 per year. To put this into
perspective, the real estate in the Talley estate sold for prices
ranging from $3.00 to $6.00 per acre, so every year the mill
brought in the equivalent of the sale of over 100 acres of land.
However, it did not happen easily.

The miller claimed he had not received credit for some payments he had made to the widow rather than the commissioner, and there were receipts for a great many repairs to the mill he had made and for which he claimed credit. All of these issues had to be resolved by the commissioner and court, and commissioner's fees and attorney fees increased with every issue, pleading, and hearing. This must have been a wonderful time to be an attorney, for if one could get a couple of these cases, he was guaranteed an income stream for the next 25 or 30 years.

As an example, consider the first commissioner in the creditors' suit against the Talley estate. He took the information from William Henry on debts owed to his father, got information from creditors on their claims, considered the valuation of the estate, and filed a report and accounting of several pages, for which he claimed a fee of $100. It seems reasonable until you consider that most math teachers of the day were probably capable of doing the same thing within a week's work. Teachers then made about $40 a month, so the commissioner had claimed a fee worth two and one-half months of a teacher's salary.

William Henry and his family continued to live in their family home. Because so many of the survey plats of the property are missing, I am not able to say with complete certainty exactly where the dwelling house was located, but I believe it was on the dower tract of Martha Wills Talley. In the suit papers is one of the handbills that was posted in 1905 to advertise the sale of this tract including improvements consisting "of a dwelling house and the usual outbuildings."

Again it is from Cousin Rosa Albert that we get an update on the homeplace. The dwelling identified above was "a small but comfortable house that replaced the much grandeur (sic) home of her uncle and aunt, Dr. Horace and Martha Talley." She estimated that the first home burned down between 1885 and 1890. Horace and Martha are buried on the property, but a later owner did not relish the idea of a cemetery on his property and located his hog pen on the hallowed ground. The hogs eventually rooted up and covered the tombstones, so the location of the graves is presently unknown.

Fluvanna Surveyor

Now back to William Henry's daybook in which it appears initially that his sole occupation was farming. Later in the book he also mentions talking to others about arrangements for their working portions of his farm on shares. I suspect by then he was finding that farming would not meet the need of the family for cash income. I am sure he thought through what job skills he possessed, and what he could do with them. He had his teaching background, but he also had engineering training at Virginia Military Institute, that would allow him to be a surveyor. William Henry Talley was appointed the Surveyor of Fluvanna County by the Court, and for many years signed his plats with the designation "S.F.C."

Over forty years ago, I learned real estate law from an attorney who was then over eighty years of age, and had learned to be careful and cautious about every detail. He did not just accept a metes and bounds description of property because it came from a surveyor. He platted out each description to see if it "closed." This means that you take each direction and distance called for in the survey and draw it to scale on a piece of paper. The survey "closed" if you end up at the spot where you began. Not all of them do, especially the older ones, but all of William Henry's that I checked over the years did close.

WHT's Saddlebag with contents

WHT's 1870 Compass with sights attached

William Henry had a kit of surveying instruments that largely fit into two saddlebags. This kit contained a surveying compass with sights on it to take bearings. The compass had a fitting on the bottom that mated to a fitting on the top of a "Jacob's Staff" which was a staff with a pointed end that could be pushed into the ground. It had a ball and socket fitting on top that was like a human hip where the ball on top of the femur fits into the socket in the pelvis. This allowed the surveyor to level his compass and then rotate it to take bearings. The Jacob's Staff would not fit into the saddlebags but could be strapped to the saddle. The saddlebags also contained the metal "chain" made of steel wire links with a total length of sixty-six feet. The chain has 100 links, so each link is 7.92" in length. These seem odd figures as we might expect a chain of 50 or 100 feet would be easier to use in computations. However, our system of measuring land in acres and distances in miles is somewhat archaic, and the chain fits into that system. There are 80 chains (80x66=5,280) in a mile. An acre is 10 square chains, or an area 66 feet by 660 feet (66x660=43,560 square feet), so chain measurement was actually fairly easy for surveyors of the time to work.

The saddlebags also contained a number of carefully prepared wooden stakes about a foot long and pointed on one end with a small hole drilled near the other end and colored yarn tied through the hole to make them more visible. These had been carefully scraped or sanded smooth. There was also a larger piece of wood that was used as a mallet to drive the stakes in the ground. Because William Henry died unexpectedly, his surveying instruments were still in his saddlebags, where they remain to this day, over a century later.

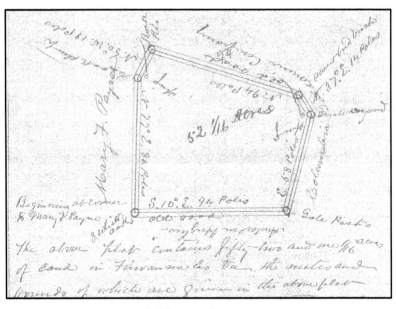

Goldmine Company

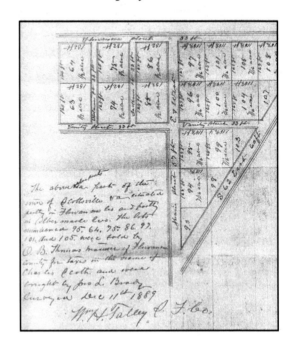

WHT Plat

Politician and More

William Henry Talley was active in politics. He served as Judge of Elections, and for over 25 years was the secretary of the local Democratic Party. In the period 1898-1902, he went to Richmond to work as a clerk for the General Assembly. He apparently liked politics in Richmond and declared himself a candidate for the legislature in 1903. He had considered running for some time, as among his effects was a letter dated 4 January 1901, from John T. Loving, Mayor of the Town of Pulaski:

Dear Friend, Yours of the 2ⁿᵈ came to hand this morning and I have written Col. Mann this morning who is one of the best fellows in the world who will help you if he possibly can do so. Nothing would give me more pleasure than to spend 45 days in the Capitol with you in the shank of winter.

In a letter dated 12 June 1903 to Joseph Anderson, a V.M.I. alumnus in Goochland, William Henry wrote:

By the way, Joe, I am a candidate for the House of Delegates to represent Fluvanna & Goochland. Can't you help me out—it is our time now. Many of my friends here are so anxious for me to become a candidate that I have decided to do so. I am the senior Democratic Secretary in the State having served the party for more than 25 years and have never asked for an office as a crumb of the spoils—anything that you can do for me will be highly appreciated and if elected will try to serve the people faithfully—I am a Confederate soldier, one who served with Mosby before I was old enough to be forced in the service, which I think should be recognized to my credit. If I get the nomination I will be in your county sometimes and will call to see you. I have not been able to visit you as I promised you sometime since I expect to be in the neighborhood of Goochland C. H. next week to do some surveying—if I had the time would spend a night with you then but will be very much hurried on this trip.

I have been unable to find any record of William Henry as a candidate for the Virginia House of Delegates, so it appears he did not get the Democratic nomination. However, his community service of another nature is documented by Jerry Holloway in *The Churches of Fluvanna County, Virginia*. William Henry was a religious man and a faithful member of Bethel Church. He served this Baptist congregation as a deacon, superintendent of the Sunday school, and a member of the committee that wrote the church history.

Bethel Church

When a Camp of Confederate Veterans formed in
Palmyra in 1896, William Henry joined. Above is a photo of
one of the meetings, and he is immediately recognizable (*bottom
left, just below the "X"*) as he seems to be the only one smiling
among a sea of steely-eyed old men. When you consider the
horrors that these men had witnessed and endured, their
unwillingness to smile for the camera is understandable.

(Left)   *Confederate Veterans'*
Reunion Ribbon

(Below) *Confederate Monument*

Home Life

As the nineteenth century had drawn to a close, the obligations that had tied William Henry to his family seem to have lessened. His sister Eliza moved to the District of Columbia, married, and worked in the Treasury Department. She often returned to Fluvanna. His brother Horace had graduated from medical school and gone to the Wentzville, Missouri area west of Saint Louis to practice medicine. Still in Fluvanna his sister Mattie had married Dr. O. M. Smith and lived nearby. His sister Mary (Mollie) was a maiden lady who eventually had her own home after staying with William Henry and his mother.

William Henry absolutely worshipped his mother, who would have had no income or home if he had not provided it. He was always very solicitous of her welfare and happiness, and made himself available to carry her to visit friends, family, church, or wherever else she wished, and when he was away on surveying jobs he always arranged for someone else to stay with her.

Martha Wills Talley

And what of this mother William Henry loved so much and for whose comfort he worked and sacrificed while he fought to keep her in her own home? Martha Wills Talley, according to her niece, Rosa Albert:

> . . . radiated fun and laughter, and was loved by everybody. She loved children and had such an

understanding heart that we instinctively went to her with our childish grievances . . . many are the sprains, bee stings, stone bruises, and tummy aches she cured.

Rosa also remembered that her aunt served the "best things to eat" both at her home and for dinner on the grounds at Bethel Church. She wrote that Aunt Tody was "the center of hospitality" at the church and invited others to join her family for Brunswick stew and roasted sweet potatoes. She cut "the most beautiful designs on watermelon rinds and cooked them into what she called 'sweetmeats,' for which she was known far and wide."

William Henry had achieved many things, but there was one thing he had not done in the first fifty-two years of his life: he had not taken a bride. He had girl friends or "flames" as he referred to them, but he had made no overtures of marriage. However, one of the young women (Annie Scott Collins) he had asked to stay with his mother had a sister named Mary Elizabeth Collins, and he became quite smitten with her. She was a daughter of William L. and Sallie Palmore Collins, and the family lived at Springfield Farm on Central Plains Road a few miles from Ingleside.

William Henry's sisters, Mary and Eliza, had some misgivings about the idea of his marrying a woman young enough to be his daughter. Fortunately, he only cared about the opinion of his mother, which was favorable, and he undertook to woo and marry this young lady. She kept his love letters, which I have read, and I can assure you that the man could write a love letter. We will respect their privacy and not quote from them, except for an early letter where he addressed the obvious age disparity. In this letter he addressed Mary Collins with a pet name:

Dear Vinie,

While sitting in the parlor at Mrs. Kie's waiting to be sent to Fork Union where I will meet Judge S(hepherd). I can but put a few of my thoughts on paper and let her who fills my whole heart read them. Now dear girl you may think as some do that I am too old to love one so young and fair as you are—or you may not, as you know of many instances where parties are happy when there is just as much difference as there is between us. You know that I idolize you and will always be willing to make any sacrifice for your happiness. I have been able for a long time to control my feelings and not tell you—but the more I see of you the stronger grows my love—and while others talk of and recommend other fellows to you it strikes like a dagger through my heart—and I can't be quiet. You know all I say is true, and I can but believe we might be happy—if you care anything for me let me know, if not, tell me for the suspense is too great.

Let others think as they may, this matter concerns only you and I. Mother loves you and when you are absent so often speaks of you & to keep her from suspicioning me of anything more than a brotherly love for you I have often said to her, "She is too young", but I love you too ardently, it would be wrong to try to smother it up as brotherly affection—Yes, I think of you in the day and dream of you at night. Do I love in vain? Can't you find in your heart

Capt. W. H. Talley and Mary Collins Talley

Talley.   Collins.

Mr. and Mrs. Wm. L. Collins

respectfully invite you to be present

at the marriage of their daughter,

Mary E.

to

Capt. William H. Talley,

at

Bethel Church, Fluvanna County, Virginia,

on

Wednesday, November the Twent=first, Nineteen Hundred,

Two o'clock P. M.

a tender spot for me? Can't you look over a few years' difference in our ages, when you know that one loves you as I do, and is willing to devote the rest of his life to making your happiness his study & if so tell me and we will try to keep it to ourselves until the time for making such things public to the whole world. If not in your power, that you have placed your affections in another, tell me, for if I am to be denied the greatest desire of my life, let me know. I stole some lilies—you are my sweet lily—these are sweet but to me not half as sweet as you are.

I believe this letter was delivered with the lilies and received a favorable reception from the young lady, as she kept it and the others that followed. The account of their wedding in the *Midland Virginian* follows:

COLLINS-TALLEY: At Bethel Church in Fluvanna County, Virginia, a Wednesday evening, November the 21ˢᵗ, 1900, at 2 o'clock, Miss Mollie E. Collins and Capt. W. H. Talley were married by Dr. Geo. H. Snead.

The entire ceremony was beautiful, solemn, impressive, attractive. The effect was greatly magnified by all the environments. The pretty decorations of the church were rendered the more beautiful by the mellowed light of numerous wax candles so arranged to add much to the effect. Dr. Snead's remarks were earnest, impressive and appropriate. Miss Lucy O. Snead's beautiful solo just preceding the wedding march lent a charm to the enchanting hour.

The church was filled with an assembly of the oldest and the youngest from all the country round about and all manifested a more than usual interest in the occasion by reason of their interest in the contracting parties. This was particularly shown by the hush—the stillness—and earnest and intent watchfulness on every face as the prospective twain with their attendants passed up the respective aisles, keeping time to the beautiful strains of music rendered by Miss Willie Shepherd.

The attendants were as follows: ushers, Wm. M. Adams, Leslie G. Attkisson; second waiters, Miss Mary D. Cash and Benj. A. Morris; best man, Judge J. O. Shepherd; maid of honor, Miss Annie Scott Collins.

We cannot close our account of this most pleasing ceremony without noticing the part taken by Samuel Cooper, who claimed the privilege of taking "the boss" to the church and carrying him and his bride home behind his own team—which is a fine and fast one. The writer saw no one more pleased and gratified on this felicitous occasion than Samuel Cooper.

All the world loves a lover, but all this section seemed to be moved with more than ordinary gratification at the happiness of the captain.

William Henry and his bride returned to live at Ingleside with his mother, whose health was declining. He continued for a couple of years after his marriage to work as a clerk in the state legislature and to work as a surveyor. On 25 January 1901 he wrote from the St. Claire Hotel and Valentine House in Richmond:

I arrived here this morning at 8:40 and after strolling around to the different hotels shaking hands with friends and old acquaintances, went over to the Capitol to see my friends then went up to my old room and went to work in my old place with some of the old clerks ... My old friends all seem very glad to see me back, especially Mr. John T. Loving—and let me tell you all compliment me on being married. John T. said I should have been married twenty-five years ago, said if I had been I would now be the finest looking man in Va., that he had never seen anyone so much improved in so short a time in all his life.

In a letter dated 12 June 1903 to Joseph Anderson, William Henry gave a quick update of his situation:

Dear Old Classmate, Your letter came to hand last night. I assure you that I appreciate such letters for they take me back to the days of my youth—many and sad have been the changes since then. Reading your letter caused me to scan more closely than I had done the V.M.I. catalogue where I find so many of our old boys have passed away, and in my own family since then Father has gone and mother has been confined to her bed for nearly 18 months—but all has not been sadness, for I took mother's advice about 3 years ago and married one of the sweetest women in all the land, but still misfortune followed me for our first born a fine boy only lived about 12 hours—but like Job I am still believing in and trusting to a wiser one than any human; one who is too wise to err and too good to be unkind. Excuse me for any personal allusions, I can't help it at times.

Martha Wills Talley died sometime between 1903 and 1905. William Henry died on 15 October 1910, and the next day the *Daily Progress* carried the death notice "Capt. W. H. Talley Dead" and continued that "Capt. W. H. Talley died at his home here early this morning, after a very brief illness." Besides relating the funeral arrangements and the names of survivors, the article continued: "Captain Talley was one of the best known men in the county, having held several county offices at different times. He was for many years County Surveyor and at one time a candidate for the House of Representatives."

Judge Shepherd's wife, Blanche Loving Shepherd, was the author of the memorial article written by "A Friend" that appeared in the 2 January 1912 issue of the *Midland Virginian*. I believe that she got most of her factual information correct, but more importantly, she captured the essence of his life: a life of devotion to duty and service to others.

IN MEMORY OF CAPT. W. H. TALLEY

Born in Cumberland county, December 19, 1847, came with his parents, Dr. H. A. and Mattie Q. Talley, to Fluvanna in 1859.

Captain Talley was a member of Co. D. 43rd battalion of cavalry, Mosby's Command, with which he served until the close of the war. Was a student at the V.M.I., entering in 1867 and graduating in 1870. Was professor of Mathematics at Shreveport, La. 1870-71, 1871-72 served as assistant professor of Latin, Mathematics and Commander of Cadets, Texas Military Institute. He served in this and other institutions in Texas until 1878 when he was called home by the death of his father; this was indeed a crisis in his life and career. On the one side a big salary, congenial work, and useful career and constant promotion, on the other was duty to mother and dependent family consisting of a widowed sister and two children, another sister, a young girl just verging into womanhood, an infant brother and sister. Owing to the kindness of his father his estate was in a bankrupt condition.

How many young men would have made this sacrifice? Would they not have argued, I can send them a part or all of my salary and thus do them more good? But not so with this scion of southern chivalry. He thought the comfort of mother, the rearing of these young children could be better accomplished by the personal sacrifice upon his part. Through his efforts his younger sister and brother were enabled to attain a collegiate education, the latter graduated with the degree of M. D.

In his rural life we find him in great demand at all social functions, picnics, reunions of old soldiers and Sunday schools he was a leader.

All classes in distress found in him a great sympathizer and able counselor and ready helper, thus sacrificing valuable time which could have been used to his personal emolument. His horses were often taken from the plow to accommodate some unfortunate neighbor.

Captain Talley served his political party faithfully and well as secretary of the Democratic Executive Committee for years, in that capacity, fearlessly defending the people against fraud and deception where ever he found it. He held this position at the time of his death, October 15, 1910.

On November 21, 1900, he married Miss Mary Elizabeth Collins. This union was blessed with three children, two of whom, viz, William Alfred Smith* and Virginia Quarles survive him.

He was buried with military honors at Bethel church October 17, 1910, and over a greater heros body was never cannon fired, for he lived a life of sacrifices for others.

A Friend

---

* Although it is also on my birth certificate, my father W. A. Talley, Sr. did not include *Smith* in his name.

Reflections

Now that over a hundred years have passed since the death of William Henry Talley, we should have a better perspective on his life. Two things stand out. The first is his decision to return to Fluvanna and do his best to care for his mother and siblings. The second is the creditors' suit. These two things combined to cause him to suspend the normal course of his life for over 30 years. He was a very religious man, and it was his Christian duty to care for his mother. He undertook that obligation without hesitation or complaint.

He supported his younger siblings as best he could, but I have no reason to believe either of them ever offered to help him support their mother or repay him for their education. He never protested except when it was reported that his sister Mary (or Mollie) said something disparaging about his decision to wed, he wrote that he could not accept her lack of gratitude after he had supported her for twenty years, and he determined to pray that she would see the error of her ways.

As for the creditors' suit, it is hard to imagine a greater waste of resources for all parties. Any lawsuit creates stress and uncertainty for the parties, but to be involved in one for thirty years that had as its object the sale of your home must have been an unbelievable stress. By the time they dragged it out for thirty years and the commissioners and lawyers got their share, I am sure the creditors received far less than full payment, and the family had no real estate. Of course, we all know that common sense in lawsuits is a rare commodity.

William Henry achieved his primary goal of taking care of his mother, but the cost to him was great. He died without a sizable estate, as he never owned any real estate in his own name.

He left behind a young widow with two dependent children. Fortunately, Mary Collins Talley was able to come up with a plan to support herself and her family. She purchased a lot in the village of Palmyra and built a large house in 1912, where she took in boarders up until almost 1950. She never remarried and apparently cherished the memory of William Henry as she kept his letters, survey notes, instruments, and pictures and other memorabilia until her death in 1954. Their graves are side by side in the C. E. Jones Cemetery at Bethel Church.

SOURCES

Black, Robert W. *Ghost, Thunderbolt, and Wizard* (2008).

Clerk's Office Records, Cumberland County Circuit Court. _____, Fluvanna County Circuit Court: especially the papers in the suits Thomas H. Perkins, et al. v. Wm. H. Talley, et al.

Cumberland County, Virginia and Its People, Cumberland County Historical Society (1985).

Evans, Thomas J. and Moyer, James M. *Mosby's Confederacy* (1991).

Fluvanna Historical Society Publications: No. 44 (Miyagawa, 1987), No. 63-64 (Miyagawa, ed., 1997).

History of St. Charles County, Missouri (1765-1885). Originally published 1885; 1997 reprint credited to Paul K. Hollrah. Included among biographical sketches of "prominent citizens" is John A. Talley. Hoarse [Horace] Talley is also mentioned.

Holloway, Jerry. *The Churches of Fluvanna County* (1966).

"James Family Papers, 1865-1927," Briscoe Center for American History, University of Texas at Austin. Collection documents the careers and many achievements of three brothers – Charles, John, and Fleming James – who moved from Virginia to Texas after the Civil War.

Jinks, Roy G. *History of Smith & Wesson* (1977).

Keen, Hugh C. and Horace Mewborn. *43rd Battalion Virginia Cavalry Mosby's Command* (1993).

Miyagawa, Ellen (ed.). *Gravestone Inscriptions, Church and Private Cemeteries in Fluvanna County, Virginia* (1994).

Official Register, 1899-1900, Virginia Military Institute, Lexington, Virginia. This copy of the catalog belonged to William Henry Talley, now in possession of the author. The publication included an alumni roster.

Register of Former Cadets, Memorial Edition (1957), Virginia Military Institute, Lexington, Virginia.

"William Henry Talley" folder, Archives of the Virginia Military Institute, Lexington.

"University of Pennsylvania Medical Department Matriculants, 1806-1852," Penn University Archives and Records Center.

West, Sue Roberson. *Buckingham Female Collegiate Institute* (1990).

Wert, Jeffrey D. *Mosby's Rangers* (1990).

APPENDIX

Choice of Weapons: John Singleton Mosby felt very strongly that the caliber .44 Colt revolver was the most suitable weapon for his Rangers, although he himself is reported to have carried the smaller caliber (.36) Colt Navy revolvers. Early in the Civil War, the Northern cavalry was generally equipped with sabers and single shot carbines, although as the war progressed, more cavalry units received repeating carbines. Mosby had no use for sabers, feeling their best use was for roasting meat over a fire. Mosby preferred to charge the enemy and either ride through their ranks while firing or to engage them at such close quarters that the Union cavalry could not effectively swing their sabers or deploy the carbines. Each Ranger carried at least two revolvers on his belt and often had a couple more in holsters fastened to the saddle or pushed into his boot where he could reach it while in the saddle. Having from twelve to twenty-four or more rounds of instantly available firepower gave the Rangers a great advantage in most instances. I never understood why the Colt revolver was chosen when the Remington 1861 Army version of the 1858 Remington was also .44 caliber and seems to be a better design. The Remington had an enclosed top over the cylinder, making it a much stronger frame than the open top Colt.

I have possession of an 1861 Remington Navy revolver that was found in the vicinity of the Palmyra Mills by my father about 1915. He went to feed the hogs and found that they had rooted up the rusty frame of this weapon. I cleaned it and found that I could read the serial number and initials scratched into the brass trigger guard. The wooden grips had rotted off. Units of Sheridan's cavalry burned the mills, and I had hopes that

1861 Remington Navy Revolver

this weapon would identify which unit, and possibly which soldier had lost it. Generally, the military maintains records of which weapons are assigned to which unit, and perhaps the initials would only belong to one soldier in that unit. Eugene and Linda Solyntjes, authors of *The Search for Corporal Dow* (2006), report that the Union purchased over 7,000 of this model. The serial number of my frame would place it about late 1861 or early 1862 manufacture date, but unfortunately other "records for this model have been lost or destroyed." The frame is missing its mainspring, so it may be that the mainspring broke, making the weapon inoperable, and it was discarded.

At any rate, the best weapon is of no use to the soldier that cannot use it. Mosby's men were proficient with their revolvers. Ranger John Munson related that it was common practice for a Ranger to ride at full gallop at a tree and put three bullets into the trunk as he passed.

Unfortunately, I have no idea what became of the Colt revolvers William Henry had when he rode with Mosby. His widow saved his wooden Confederate drum canteen, which has been lost, but I have his Smith and Wesson pocket pistol. I remember when I was first shown the pistol by my aunt (Virginia

Quarles Talley) about 1970. It is a .22 short caliber and carries patent dates of April 3, 1855, July 5, 1859, and December 16, 1860 on the barrel. The dates, the shape of the grip (called a bird's head grip), and the fact the frame is made of iron rather than the earlier brass frames all identify this as a Model 1, Third Issue, which began production in 1868 with serial no. 1, and continued until 1882 with serial no. 131, 163 (Roy G. Jinks, *History of Smith & Wesson*, 1977). The serial number would place it about midway of the production. Therefore, we know this pistol was acquired by William Henry after the war. When I opened the pistol and saw that six of the seven cylinders were still loaded with .22 short cartridges, my aunt turned quite pale, as she said she had no idea it was still loaded and had pointed it at people in play. Actually, the pistol is still loaded, as the brass or copper cartridges have corroded in the iron cylinder, and despite soaking them in every solvent available, I have never been able to remove them.

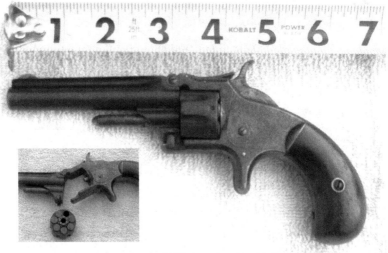

Smith and Wesson Pocket Pistol

INDEX

78